Mary Bucklin Davenport Claflin

Personal Recollections of John G. Whittier

Mary Bucklin Davenport Claflin

Personal Recollections of John G. Whittier

ISBN/EAN: 9783337217402

Printed in Europe, USA, Canada, Australia, Japan

Cover: Foto ©Thomas Meinert / pixelio.de

More available books at **www.hansebooks.com**

PERSONAL RECOLLECTIONS

OF

JOHN G. WHITTIER

BY

MARY B. CLAFLIN

NEW YORK: 46 East 14th Street
THOMAS Y. CROWELL & CO.
BOSTON: 100 Purchase Street

COPYRIGHT, 1893,
BY T. Y. CROWELL & CO.

Typography by J. S. Cushing & Co.
Presswork by S. J. Parkhill & Co.

PREFACE.

My reverent sense of the power and purity and beauty of Mr. Whittier's life, and of his wide and salutary influence, has led me to a diffident attempt to give to those who have not had the privilege of his intimate acquaintance, a glimpse of him as I knew him.

In the poem, "The Morning Star," published here for the first time, Miss Edna Dean Proctor has embodied his almost life-long plaint of sleepless nights, and the gladness with which he hailed the dawn.

M. B. C.

May, 1893.

THE MORNING STAR.

(JOHN GREENLEAF WHITTIER, died at dawn, Sept. 7, 1892.)

"How long and weary are the nights," he said,
"When thought and memory wake, and sleep has fled;
When phantoms from the past the chamber fill,
And tones, long silent, all my pulses thrill;
While, sharp as doom, or faint in distant towers,
Knell answering knell, the chimes repeat the hours,
And wandering wind and waning moon have lent
Their sighs and shadows to the heart's lament.
Then, from my pillow looking east, I wait

The dawn; and life and joy come back,
    elate,
When, fair above the seaward hill afar,
Flames the lone splendor of the morning
    star."

O Vanished One! O loving, glowing heart!
When the last evening darkened round thy
    room,
Thou didst not with the setting moon depart;
Nor take thy way in midnight's hush and
    gloom;
Nor let the wandering wind thy comrade be,
Outsailing on the dim, unsounded sea —
The silent sea where falls the muffled oar,
And they who cross the strand return no
    more;
But thou didst wait, celestial deeps to try,
Till dawn's first rose had flushed the paling
    sky,
And pass, serene, to life and joy afar,
Companioned by the bright and morning
    star!

EDNA DEAN PROCTOR.

PERSONAL RECOLLECTIONS

OF

JOHN G. WHITTIER

PERSONAL RECOLLECTIONS

OF

JOHN G. WHITTIER.

EMERSON felicitously says, "the ornament of a house is the friends who frequent it."

The house where Mr. Whittier was a guest was ornamented indeed; for a more genial, suggestive, inspiring friend, or one with a more distinct personality, has rarely given the blessing and benediction of his presence to any home, and the family fortunate enough to have him with them at the fireside, counted themselves especially favored and enriched. He was unique in his absolute simplicity and truthfulness — the simplicity and truthfulness of clear conviction and sturdy strength, and of a nature that in its tenderness and justice seemed to reflect the very heart of God.

Mr. Whittier was responsive to every appeal, whether of joy or sorrow, as his hearty laugh, his "smartly smitten knee," at some amusing story, or his burst of righteous indignation, at a tale of injustice and wrong, plainly showed. As intense in nature, as he was sagacious, though ordinarily shy and cautious and reserved, he could, under favorable conditions, blossom into rare graciousness and sympathy of speech and manner. Those who have sat with him of an evening, in a quiet firelit room, will never forget his charming vivacity and pleasant confidences, alternating with dreamy silence and repose.

He never led, but always waited for

some one to begin the conversation, yet once launched upon some topic that interested him, he would talk for an hour with an enthusiasm and spontaneity and sprightliness that would surprise one who had only seen him in his silent moods. But his feelings were so strong upon the subjects which had engrossed his attention, that an hour's conversation would utterly exhaust him. One day after talking with a friend of whom he was fond, and into whose morbid feelings he had entered deeply, he exclaimed after she had left — "There! I will not go down into the depths with M—— again; it makes my head spin. The next time she comes I'll talk about the fashions."

Born on a hilly, rocky New England farm, where the struggle for daily bread was hard, and where there was little to cultivate the imagination or encourage his attempts at poetic flights, he still indulged his dreams, and was often so absorbed in his fancies, that he would stop in the furrow and lean upon his hoe, forgetful of all around him until his father, "a prompt, decisive man," would call out "That's enough for stand, now, John." During all this time, Nature, the old nurse, was storing his mind with a wealth of material, from which he has since drawn with lavish hand, that he might bestow it upon those whose souls are, perhaps, less keen to note her wonderful harmonies.

Meanwhile this farm life seemed dull to the boy, "possessed of the sore disquiet of a restless brain," and he began early to write the "rhymes" (he always spoke of his poems as "my rhymes") which have since given so much pleasure to the world. But when he espoused the cause of human freedom, and entered the despised ranks of the Abolitionists, it was not easy to find a publisher for his poems. He said to a young friend, who was about publishing his first book, under the happiest auspices, "Thee is fortunate to find a publisher so soon. I could find no one to publish my first book, and, for that matter, I had to wait many years."

Our poet early learned, in a severe school, what self-sacrifice meant — how great a sacrifice let any one with "the scholar's heart aflame," imagine. He was an active partaker in the struggles of his country; with him duty was commanding, and he always kept before him and acted upon the idea that

"Beyond the poet's sweet dream lives
The eternal epic of the man."

When he was about twenty-one he made his first visit to Boston which was an occasion of sufficient importance for him to make a change in his dress. The buttons on his coat, before this of home manufacture, were now made of "lasting," bought from the village store. With his new attire he arrived in the city, where he describes himself, with great amusement, watching the crowds as they passed up and down the street, and wondering if any one noticed his "boughten buttons."

It was at this time that he became the owner and purchaser of a book of his own selection, a copy of Shakespeare, which he says he carried home under his arm with a consciousness of riches untold, although he was quite ignorant of the nature of his treasure. Previous to this a stray copy of Burns had taught him to detect "the beautiful in the common," and made him feel it possible to write the songs that have since shown "through all familiar things, the romance underlying." One of his earliest publications was "Legends of New England," legends which he tells us his mother taught her children, —

> "While she turned her wheel,
> Or run the new knit stocking heel,
> Recalling, in her fitting phrase,
> So rich and picturesque and free,
> The common unrhymed poetry
> Of simple life and country ways,
> The story of her early days."

Before this he had somewhere found a volume of Scott's "Pirate," and he and his sister had enjoyed the stolen luxury of reading it late at night, until they had exhausted the tallow dip, and at a critical point in the story had to retire ignominiously in the dark. Novels were under a ban in the Quaker household, hence the necessity for secrecy. The sister, whom he thus mentions, was his constant companion. To him her shy, beautiful soul opened like a flower in the warmth of social communion. He says of her she —

> "held herself apart
> Of all she saw, and let her heart
> Against the household bosom lean."

* * * * *

> "Yet following me where'er I went
> With dark eyes full of love's content."

* * * * *

> "I cannot feel that thou art far
> Since near at need the angels are;
> And when the sunset gates unbar
> Shall I not see thee waiting stand,
> And white against the evening star
> The welcome of thy beckoning hand."

In "The Tent on the Beach" we find a portrait of himself at this era of his life drawn by his own modest hand: —

"And one there was, a dreamer born,
  Who, with a mission to fulfil,
Had left the Muses' haunts to turn
  The crank of an opinion-mill;
Making his rustic reed of song
A weapon in the war with wrong,
Yoking his fancy to the breaking-plough,
That beam-deep turned the soil for truth to spring and grow."

Mr. Whittier's attachment to his own sect — "Our Folks," as he always called the Friends — was strong, and he disapproved of any change in their habits or in their methods of worship.

When asked once why the Quakers so perverted the English grammar, his reply was : "It has been the manner of speech of my people for two hundred years ; it was my mother's language, and it is good enough for me; I shall not change my grammar." Coming from a Quaker meeting one day in a state of great indignation, he said, "Our folks have got to talking t' much; they even want a glass of water on the table, and some of them want singing in the meetings. I tell them if they want singing, they have got to get the world's folks to do it for them, for two hundred years of silence have taken all the sing out of our people."

He loved a simple song sung by a friend, and when he was asked, "Do you like that, Mr. Whittier?" he was careful how he expressed much interest, because that would not be in accordance with Quaker notions. His reply usually was, "Thy voice is very sweet." I think he often felt like the children in the family of an English Quaker where Mr. Gough was visiting. One day Mr. Gough sang a comic song, in his inimitable manner, which greatly delighted the children. The next day, wishing to have a repetition of the fun, they said, "John Gough, will thee tell us that same story thee told us yesterday, in the same tone of voice?" Mr. Whittier often wanted the little song told "in the same tone of voice," when some sweet young girl had sung to him a Scotch ballad. He was very fond of Scotch stories, whether told in song or on the printed page.

Mr. Whittier was tall and erect to the last, in spite of his eighty-four years. His hair was frosted, his eyes were dark and piercing, and quick to note everything that passed before them. His dress was black, and made after the most approved fashion of the Quakers. His coat was a perfect fit, and his outside garment, with its fine fur collar, was very becoming, which fact his friends sometimes suspected he understood as well as they.

He was sensitive to every change of temperature, and seemed to be constantly longing for the summer air, the blooming flowers, and the singing birds. He suffered in the cold, bleak winds of New England, and often said, " It must be confessed we have a hard climate. I always wish the Pilgrims had drifted down to Virginia." But his love for Massachusetts and for Essex County was greater than his dislike of the long winters and the rough gales. The sunniest climes and the richest landscapes could not win him from his loyalty to his home, for he found every charm of beauty and grandeur in its rugged scenes. The Merrimac was more to him than the Rhine, and Chocorua and Mount Washington more than the splendors of the Jungfrau and the Matterhorn. Not the Bay of Naples nor the Bosphorus could rival in his affections the North Shore, and the expanse of foam-crested waters about the Isles of Shoals. A friend whom he greatly admired, in answering some inquiries of his as to her birthplace in another State, added, " but my ancestors lived in Manchester-by-the-Sea." — " Oh," he exclaimed, "I knew thee was from Essex County."

These extracts from "The Merrimac," "The Hill-top" and "The Wreck of Rivermouth," show his enthusiastic love for the wind-swept hills and coasts of his own land: —

" O child of that white-crested mountain whose springs
Gush forth in the shade of the cliff-eagle's wings,
Down whose slopes to the lowlands thy wild waters shine,
Leaping gray walls of rock, flashing through the dwarf pine."

* * * * *

"I felt the cool breath of the North;
　Between me and the sun,
O'er deep, still lake, and ridgy earth,
　I saw the cloud-shades run.
Before me, stretched for glistening miles,
　Lay mountain-girdled Squam;
Like green-winged birds, the leafy isles
　Upon its bosom swam.

　　＊　　＊　　＊　　＊　　＊

"There towered Chocorua's peak; and west,
　Moosehilleck's woods were seen,
With many a nameless slide-scarred crest
　And pine-dark gorge between.
Beyond them, like a sun-rimmed cloud,
　The great Notch mountains shone,
Watched over by the solemn-browed
　And awful face of stone!

　　＊　　＊　　＊　　＊　　＊

"So, as I sat upon Appledore
In the calm of a closing summer day,
　And the broken lines of Hampton shore
In purple mist of cloudland lay,
The Rivermouth Rocks their story told;
And waves aglow with sunset gold,
Rising and breaking in steady chime,
Beat the rhythm and kept the time.

"And the sunset paled, and warmed once more
  With a softer, tenderer after-glow;
In the east was moon-rise, with boats off-shore
  And sails in the distance drifting slow.
The beacon glimmered from Portsmouth bar,
The White Isle kindled its great red star;
And life and death in my old-time lay
Mingled in peace like the night and day!"

Mr. Whittier was a many-sided man and could adapt himself to any condition of mind. He had great warmth of affection for his friends; tenderness to the erring, and capacity for suffering with others, were marked traits in his character, — but he had always faith in ultimate good for all. He said, "Surely God would not permit his children to suffer if it were not to work out for them the highest good. For God never does, nor suffers to be done, but that which we would do if we could see the end of all events as well as He.

The little circumstance of death will make no difference with me: I shall have the same friends in that other world that I have here; the same loves and aspirations and occupations. If it were not so, I should not be myself, and surely I shall not lose my identity. God's love is so infinitely greater than mine that I cannot fear for his children, and when I long to help some poor, suffering, erring fellow-creature, I am consoled with the thought that his great heart of love is more moved than mine can be, and so I rest in peace." This is in keeping with his beautiful lines in "The Eternal Goodness."

"I know not where His islands lift
  Their fronded palms in air;
I only know I cannot drift
  Beyond His love and care."

In the companionship of his friends the poet found the keenest pleasure of his lonely life. Mr. Emerson, Mr. Sumner, Edna Dean Proctor, Harriet Beecher Stowe, Elizabeth Stuart Phelps, Lydia Maria Child, Mr. and Mrs. James T. Fields,— Mrs. Fields he characterized as "a sweet flower of Christian womanhood," — were among his most cherished friends.

With Mr. Emerson he discussed the great problems of human needs, and the great mysteries of eternity.

With Elizabeth Stuart Phelps his favorite theme was the occupations of heaven. They would sit — their two heads together — over the dying embers, at the twilight hour, and talk of what they should require to satisfy their souls in heaven. He said to her one day, "Elizabeth, thee would not be happy in heaven unless thee could go missionary to the other place, now and then."

With Mrs. Stowe he would sit till the small hours of the morning, and till the lights burned blue, to talk about psychical mysteries, and relate stories of ghosts and spirit rappings and manifestations. They "wooed the courteous ghosts" together; but he said, "Much as I have wooed them, they never appear to me. Mrs. Stowe is more fortunate — the spirits sometimes come at her bidding, but never at mine — and what wonder? It would be a foolish spirit that did not prefer her company to that of an old man like me." They would repeat the most marvellous stories of ghostly improbabilities, apparently, for the time being, believing every word.

With Miss Proctor he talked of poetry, and especially of Oriental poetry and religion, which had a wonderful fascination for him; of Egypt and the

East; of the Mohammedans and their worship; and of the imposing ceremonies of the Greek Church in Russia. Once, when he expressed his delight at some description she had given him of Moscow, she said, "You should go there yourself, Mr. Whittier." — "Oh, no," he answered; "there's no need of that. I can see it all, when thee tells it."

Mr. Whittier had great pleasure in conversing with Mr. Emerson; and he often repeated the conversations they had in their brief and infrequent visits together. In driving, one day, Mr. Emerson pointed out a small, unpainted house by the roadside, and said, "There lives an old Calvinist in that house, and she says she prays for me every day. I am glad she does. I pray for myself."

"Does thee?" said Mr. Whittier. "What does thee pray for, friend Emerson?"

"Well," replied Mr. Emerson, "when I first open my eyes upon the morning meadows, and look out upon the beautiful world, I thank God that I am alive, and that I live so near Boston."

In one of their conversations, Mr. Emerson remarked that the world had not yet seen the highest development of manhood.

"Does thee think so?" said Mr. Whittier. "I suppose thee would admit that Jesus Christ is the highest development our world has seen?"

"Yes, yes; but not the highest it will see."

"Does thee think the world has yet reached the ideals the Christ has set for mankind?"

"No, no," said Mr. Emerson; "I think not."

"Then is it not the part of wisdom to be content with what has been given us, till we have lived up to that ideal? And when we need something higher, Infinite Wisdom will supply our needs."

He told the story of a dear aunt, —

"The sweetest woman ever Fate
Perverse denied a household mate,"

whose experience, he said, brought him nearer to a ghost than anything that ever happened to him. This aunt was one of the family described in "Snow Bound," —

"Who, lonely, homeless, not the less,
Found peace in love's unselfishness."

She was betrothed to a young man in the village, who was called away to some remote place in the West. She waited faithfully for his return, but he did not come. One night she was sitting alone over the dying embers of the kitchen fire, while the full moon

shone outside upon the fields of snow.
As she looked from the window, she
saw approaching, on a white steed, a
horseman. She recognized her lover,
and ran to the door to meet him, with
outstretched arms, and all the ardor of
love's young dream, and lo! horse and
rider had vanished.

Days afterward, she learned that her
lover had died at that very hour, "and
for all the years thereafter 'of toil and
soil and care,' —

> "she kept her genial mood
> And simple faith of maidenhood;
>
> *   *   *   *   *
>
> All unprofaned she held apart
> The virgin fancies of the heart."

Mr. Whittier believed in following
the inner light, and when he thought
he was directed by that inner light, no
power on earth could influence him to
turn aside. If he decided to move at a

certain moment of time, nothing could induce him to change his mind; no storm was severe enough to deter him from going on the train he had set his heart on. He used to tell a story of one of his friends as an illustration of the wisdom of being guided by, and yielding to, the inner light.

"I have an old friend, he said, who followed the leadings of the spirit, and always made it a point to go to meeting on First-day. On one First-day morning, he made ready for meeting, and suddenly turning to his wife, said, 'I am not going to meeting this morning; I am going to take a walk.' His wife inquired where he was going, and he replied: 'I don't know; I am impelled to go, I know not where.' With his walking stick he started and went out of the city for a mile or two, and came to a country house that stood some distance from the road.

The gate stood open, and a narrow lane, into which he turned, led up to the house where something unusual seemed to be going on. There were several vehicles standing around the yard, and groups of people were gathered here and there. When he reached the house, he found there was a funeral, and he entered with the neighbors, who were there to attend the service. He listened to the funeral address and to the prayer. It was the body of a young woman lying in the casket before him, and he arose and said, 'I have been led by the spirit to this house; I know nothing of the circumstances connected with the death of this person; but I am impelled by the spirit to say that she has been accused of something of which she is not guilty, and the false accusation has hastened her death.'

"The friend sat down, and a murmur

of surprise went through the room. The minister arose and said, 'Are you a God or what *are* you?' The friend replied, 'I am only a poor sinful man, but I was led by the inner light to come to this house, and to say what I have said, and I would ask the person in this room who knows that the young woman, now beyond the power of speech, was not guilty of what she was accused, to vindicate her in this presence.' After a fearful pause, a woman stood up and said, 'I am the person,' and while weeping hysterically, she confessed that she had wilfully slandered the dead girl. The friend departed on his homeward way. Such," said Mr. Whittier, "was the leading of the inner light."

His modest reserve was unequalled. Once, when he was visiting us, I said to him that we enjoyed the atmosphere of the house better for having him with us:— "Even when you are in your own room I am happier for knowing that you are in the house."

The dear old man, with a heart full of affection, but unused to much expression, after hesitating a moment, said, with a good deal of feeling, "thee is a sensible woman — do n't thee talk so — I can not believe thee."

He often playfully said, at some feminine extravagance of language, "Thee is a little Oriental in thy speech."

Always ready to give sympathetic advice, his words of wisdom, coming as they did from a heart illumined by the inner light, never failed to reach the hearts of those who needed help.

The morning's mail usually brought him a great number of letters (often as many as fifty), and one morning, as he was looking over the pile before him, he lingered a long time over one, and looked troubled, as though it contained some sad news.

At length, handing it to me, he said, "I wish thee would read that letter," and then with his head down cast, and his deep, melancholy eyes looking, as it seemed, into the very depths of human mysteries, he sat till I had finished it.

It was written by one whose life had been spent on a remote farm among the hills of New Hampshire, away from every privilege her nature craved — a most pathetic letter, written, it seemed, out of the deepest human longing for sympathy, for companionship and uplifting. The lonely woman wrote, she said, to tell Mr. Whittier what his poems had been to her during all the years of her desolate heart-yearning for education, for enlightenment, and for touch with the great outside world. She added, "in my darkest moments I have found light and comfort in your poems, which I always keep by my side, and as I never expect to have the privilege of looking into your face, I feel that I must tell you, before I leave this world, what you have been through your writings to one, and I have no doubt to many a longing heart and homesick soul. I have never been in a place so dark and hopeless that I could not find light and comfort and hope in your poems, and when I go into my small room and close the door upon the worries and perplexing cares that constantly beset me, and sit down by my window that looks out over the hills which have been my only companions, I never fail to find in the volume which is always by my side, some word of peace and comfort to my longing heart."

The letter was such as to bring tears from any sympathetic heart, and I remarked, returning it to him, "I would rather have the testimony you are constantly receiving from forlorn and hungry souls — the assurance that you are helping God's neglected children — than the crown of any queen on earth."

With tearful eyes and choking voice he replied, "Such letters greatly humiliate me. I can sometimes write from a high plane, but thee knows I cannot live up to it all the time. I wish I could think I deserved the kind things said of me."

In the poem, "Brother of Mercy," Mr. Whittier gives not only an exquisite description of

"Soft sunset lights, through green Val d'Arno sifted,"

and "the Brotherhood of Mercy going on

some errand good," — a description so true that one can scarcely believe the poet never breathed the air of Italy, or looked upon the terraced hills of La Cortesa — but he expresses the deep feeling that runs through all his poems and which is a part of his very life. When he makes the Brother of Mercy say, replying to the Monk's comforting assertion that he

> "Shall sit down
> Clad in white robes, and wear a golden crown,"

"I am too poor for such grand company;
The crown would be too heavy for this gray
Old head; and God forgive me if I say
It would be hard to sit there night and day,
Like an image in the Tribune, doing naught
With these hard hands, that all my life have
  wrought,
Not for bread only, but for pity's sake.

* * * * *

"I love my fellow-men: the worst I know
I would do good to. Will death change me so

That I shall sit among the lazy saints,
Turning a deaf ear to the sore complaints
Of souls that suffer;
* * * * *
The world of pain were better, if therein
One's heart still be human, and desires
Of natural pity drop upon its fires
Some cooling tears."

His attitude was always that of one who was favored beyond his deserts.

In the poem "At Last," about which he said to me, "I do not like to give my innermost feelings to the world, but I wrote that poem because I could not help it," the same sentiment is expressed.

"No gate of pearl, no branch of palm I merit,
Nor street of shining gold."

Mr. Whittier was very reluctant to meet strangers, though every stranger of note from our own country, and from abroad, considered his visit incomplete if he did not meet Mr. Whittier. Sometimes he was so pursued by people that he was obliged to seek refuge in a quiet country corner where he could not be easily found.

On one occasion I invited some of his old acquaintances to an afternoon tea. Knowing his aversion to meeting people, and fearing he might flit, I did not speak to him of my plan, but contrived by some artifice to keep him in the house till the guests should arrive.

He was so shy that he could not be counted upon, and often, if he suspected company had been invited to meet him, he would slip away. With his keen perception and insight, he discovered that something a little out of the ordinary course was going on, and he said, " What is thee going to do ? I think thee is going to do something."

I replied, " Why do you think so, Mr. Whittier ? "

"Oh, I know thee is going to have some kind of a fandango."

When the guests came he received them most cordially, and treated them as though they were conferring a great favor upon him. After they had left, he said, with a boy's shyness, "I think thee managed that very well."

Mr. Whittier loved beautiful things, though he was careful not to express much admiration of pictures and statuary, because that would be inconsistent with his Quaker ideas. He called everything in the way of statuary, from a tiny figure to a colossal bust, "a graven image." In the house of one of his friends whom he frequently visited, there was a life-size figure of Ruth, which turned on a pivot. He was often seen examining this in private, and evidently admiring it, and he was quite disturbed one day when the figure was by accident turned in such a way as to present the back, rather than the face, to those who approached it, and he said to his hostess, " Thy graven image appears to be backing folks t' much. I think thee better turn her round."

Sleep was the one blessing that seemed to be denied him, and which he constantly longed for. He resorted to every simple remedy for insomnia — but it was all in vain — his was the " sore disquiet of a restless brain," and he would often come down in the morning looking tired and worn from his long night of wakefulness, and say, " It is of no use; the sleep of the innocent is denied me. Perhaps I do not deserve it."

The pen portrait drawn by Hayne, the Southern poet, gives, perhaps, the best idea of Mr. Whittier's personality:

" So 'neath the Quaker poet's tranquil roof,
From all deep discords of the world aloof,

I sit once more and measured converse hold,
With him whose nobler thoughts are rhythmic
   gold;
See his deep brows half-puckered in a knot,
O'er some hard problem of our mortal lot,
Or a dream soft as May winds of the South,
Waft a girl's sweetness 'round his firm set
   mouth.

"Or, should he deem wrong threats the public
   weal,
Lo, the whole man seems girt with flashing
   steel;
His glance a sword thrust and his words of ire,
Like thunder tones from some old prophet's
   lyre.
Or by the hearthstone, when the day is done,
Mark swiftly lanced a sudden shaft of fun;
The short quick laugh, the smartly smitten knees,
Are all sure tokens of a mind at ease.

"God's innocent pensioners in the woodland dim,
The fields, the pastures know and trust in him,
And in their love, his lonely heart is blest,
Our pure hale-minded Cowper of the West."

Quaker as he was, and gentle and

graceful as were his early poems, "his martial lyrics had something of the energy of a primitive bard urging on the hosts to battle."

The "silent, shy, peace-loving man became a fiery partisan," and held his intrepid way against the public frown, —

> "The ban of Church and State,
> The fierce mob's hounding down."

His poetry was as genuine, as his wrath was terrific, and many a political time-server, who was proof against Garrison's hottest denunciations, and Phillips's most stinging invectives, quailed before Whittier's smiting rhymes. Yet strange to say, the opprobium and abuse which covered them did not fall on him. The reason for this may be that in order to point a story, or round a period, he never allowed himself to swerve from the truth; and the pitying scorn which he sometimes used fell upon the head of the wrong-doer from no personal motive, but from his intense hatred of injustice and wrong. Such was the poem "Ichabod," with its burning denunciation and lofty contempt, written after Webster's 7th of March speech (1850).

> "So fallen! so lost! the light withdrawn
>   Which once he wore!
> The glory from his gray hair gone
>   Forevermore!
>
> *   *   *   *
>
> "Then pay the reverence of old days
>   To his dead fame:
> Walk backward with averted gaze
>   And hide the shame!"

But his scorn was such as an angel might have used. His unfailing charity and sweetness of spirit were shown in a remark he made not long after writing the poem: "I could wish 'Ichabod' were unwritten, except that it is a matter of history."

His early poem, "The Pine-Tree," is like the blast of a trumpet.

"Lift again the stately emblem on the Bay State's
    rusted shield,
Give to Northern winds the Pine-Tree on our
    banner's tattered field.
Sons of men who sat in council with their Bibles
    round the board
Answering England's royal missive with a firm,
    'THUS SAITH THE LORD!'
Rise again for home and freedom! set the battle
    in array!
What the fathers did of old time we their sons
    must do to-day.
  * * * * *
"Where's the Man for Massachusetts? Where's
    the voice to speak her free?
Where's the hand to light up bonfires from her
    mountains to the sea?
Beats her Pilgrim pulse no longer? Sits she
    dumb in her despair?
Has she none to break the silence? Has she
    none to do and dare?

O my God! for one right worthy to lift up her
 rusted shield,
And to plant again the Pine-Tree in her banner's
 tattered field!"

In 1840 Mr. Whittier first faced the mob and became familiar with personal danger, and in his later years he took great pleasure in fighting over his battles by the evening fireside. No one who had the privilege of listening to him, as he sat with his chosen friends in the quiet of a winter's evening, can ever forget the charm of such conversations. But if a stranger chanced to intrude upon those delectable moments, the poet's voice was immediately silenced.

In the stormy days, when every Abolitionist was a marked man, an important meeting was held in New York. Among the speakers on the platform sat Garrison, with his shining bald head, and C. C. Burleigh, whose ample locks fell down his shoulders in true poetic fashion, while above them all towered the massive head of Fred Douglas, the colored orator. As usual, the proceedings were greatly disturbed by the rioters; but in a temporary lull which chanced to occur, a high-pitched voice was heard crying, "Mr. Chairman, one word, Mr. Chairman. I have a proposition to make that will restore order." —

"What is your proposition?" quickly replied the Chairman, "let us have it."

"Let that nigger there shave Burleigh, and make a wig for Garrison, and all the difference will be settled."

Strange to say, when the audience had recovered from the burst of laughter, order was restored, and the speakers proceeded without interruption.

Mr. Whittier, being a friend of Garrison, Douglas, and Burleigh, took great delight in telling this story.

Mr. Whittier was a keen observer of all public affairs, and the trusted adviser of many of the most eminent men of the old Bay State. He seemed to have prophetic vision, and was one of the most sagacious counsellors in the State, which was then famous for its able men. How clear and far-seeing was his judgment may be seen from the fact that he was the first to suggest to our great statesman, Charles Sumner, that he should allow his name to be used in the choice for senator, and with him, as the years went by, Mr. Sumner often discussed the important issues before the country. He followed, with keen interest and discriminating insight, the action of Congress, and no smallest question escaped his close investigation. His instinct was unerring, and his political friends constantly sought his advice and counsel.

When the terrible years of the war

came, and the days were dark and the hearts of the bravest grew faint with weary waiting, he, who had so often reminded the people that no compromise with sin could be tolerated, stood ready to infuse new life into drooping souls; and as each crisis drew near, some poem, or open letter, from Mr. Whittier would arouse the people from despair, and assure them of triumph in the end; and when the end came, in the midst of the universal rejoicing, no voice rang out more joyously than his, and none was more quick to counsel forgetfulness of the strife in the new birth of the nation.

For Mr. Sumner he had great affection and admiration. He wrote, at the time the vote of censure was passed upon Mr. Sumner, "The great and general Court have acted like fools, and worse, in denouncing Charles Sumner. I begin to hate parties and politics!

"I have sent to Hon. Willard Phillips, our Representative, a draft of a petition for rescinding the odious resolution passed by the late extra session in censure of Senator Sumner. I make the movement not merely for Sumner's sake, but for the sake of the honor and good name of our dear old Commonwealth. Sumner's fame is beyond its reach, but we cannot afford the disgrace in our records. I have not found one intelligent and respectable man who approved of that resolution."

"I have just received a telegram announcing the death of our dear and noble friend Charles Sumner. My heart is too full for words. In deepest sympathy of sorrow I reach out my hands to thee and Governor Claflin who loved him so well. He has died as he wished, at his post of duty, and when the heart of his beloved Massachusetts was turning toward him with more than the old-time love and reverence. God's peace be with him."

"I have been to see Jackson's bust of Sumner. It is very grand — beautiful as the Greek Apollo — full of the character of the man, but still somewhat ideal — a little glorified. Thee knows I am no judge of graven images."

Mr. Whittier always liked to tell the story of his own political preferment. He said: "In 1835 and 36 I had two years' experience in the Massachusetts Legislature, and from that time on, for forty years, I have always been supported for that position, but without anxiety to myself till my one vote became two; then it was necessary to look about."

Mr. Whittier knew how he stood in

the literary world — none knew better. It was sometimes said he had less culture than the poets who contested with him the palm of popularity, and that there is now and then to be found an imperfect line among his verses. It may be so, but there is never an imperfect thought; and if during the forty years when others were travelling in foreign lands, rich in classic legend and story, or working quietly in their secluded libraries at home, Whittier, forgetful of himself and his fame, was expending his energies in the great cause of human freedom — do not his own words explain his high motive and his keen sense of moral responsibility? Surely

> "Never yet to Hebrew seer
> A clearer voice of duty came."

He said, "my soul spoke out against the wrong":—

"Forego thy dreams of lettered ease,
Put thou the scholar's promise by,
The rights of man are more than these,"
He heard and answered, "Here am I."
"Beyond the poet's sweet dream lives
The eternal epic of the man."

While Mr. Whittier was painfully conscious of any shortcoming in his own efforts, he was naturally sensitive to criticism. I found him one day in my library in an unusually sad and dejected state of mind. He stood before the fire, with his hands clasped behind him, looking, as it were, into space, and after a long silence he said, with a sigh: "Tennyson has written a perfect poem. It is a great thing to write a *perfect* poem. *Tennyson* is so grand."

There had been at that time an unfavorable criticism upon Whittier in an English journal. It was sometimes said that he was not appreciated in England, but in fact he was well known and greatly beloved and widely read there.

Canon Kingsley said to him, when he came to America, "Mr. Whittier, I want to tell you how much we all love you; everything you write is read in England; my wife is never without a volume of your poems by her side."

George MacDonald sent him a book through the hands of a friend, saying, "Take this book from my hands to Mr. Whittier's hand, clasped firmly as I give it to you, and tell him how much we love him in England."

When Dom Pedro, the Emperor of Brazil, was visiting Boston, he was invited one morning to a private parlor to meet some of the men who have made this city famous in the world of letters. As one after another was presented to him, he received each one graciously, but without enthusiasm. But when Mr.

Whittier's name was announced his face suddenly lighted up, and, grasping the poet's hand, he made a gesture as though he would embrace him; but seeing that to be contrary to the custom of the Friends, he passed his arm through that of Mr. Whittier's, and drew him gently to a corner where he remained with him, absorbed in conversation, until the time came to leave. The Emperor, taking the poet's hand in both his own again, bade him a reluctant farewell, and turned to leave the room, but still unsatisfied, he was heard to say, "Come with me," and they passed slowly down the staircase, his arm around Mr. Whittier.

A friend of his had the rare pleasure of spending some hours with the venerable William and Mary Howitt in Rome, and their conversation was wholly about Mr. Whittier. "Tell me," said the gentle, lovely Mary Howitt, "tell me every word you can recall that you have heard him say; and tell him when you see him, how much we love him on this side the water, and how eagerly we watch for every word that comes from his pen."

John Bright would stand with his arm upon the mantel by his own fireside, and repeat page after page of Mr. Whittier's poems. He said to an American lady who was visiting him, "I would rather see Mr. Whittier than any man in your country. If I go to America I shall seek him first."

Our own Lowell said his name was "Sweetly familiar to both Englands' ears."

Though Mr. Whittier's prevailing habit of mind was one of seriousness, he had a keen sense of the ludicrous, and was famous among his friends for his quickness of repartee. No good story ever failed to receive appreciation from him, while one in a mood for jesting found him always responsive; but the jester was obliged to sharpen his wits, or he would find himself the worse for the tilt.

On his return home one day, Mr. Whittier repeated the conversation he had had with a literary friend with whom he had been dining. He said, "My friend was downcast and sad, and I inquired what was the matter. 'Oh,' he said, 'I am getting old, and I expect soon to be called away to an unknown country. Here I am situated just as I wish to be. I live on Beacon Street, in a house that suits me; I have just the friends I want; and I do n't feel happy about being called away to that other country I know nothing about; and the worst of it is, I may have to rub against a Hottentot or a cannibal, as I pass through the pearly gates. It strikes me that the society of heaven will be rather promiscuous.'

" Do n't thee think the Beacon Street folks will have a good deal to put up with, when they get to the Celestial City?" said Mr. Whittier.

Mr. Whittier never spoke in public, and so great was his fear and dislike of being called out, that he rarely attended any large gathering; but after Mr. Sumner's death he could not refuse to pay a tribute of respect to his old friend and compeer, and he accepted an invitation to be present at a memorial service, to be held in a private parlor, upon condition that he should be allowed to remain silent. After several addresses by other friends of the great statesman, a word from Mr. Whittier was eagerly called for. Much annoyed, but without a moment's hesitation, he arose, and, amid breathless silence, told the story of a Scotch colonel, who, being interred with military honors, had an unfriendly regiment detailed to fire a salute over his grave, seeing which, an on-looker said, "If the colonel could have known this, he would not have died." — "So I feel," said Mr. Whittier. "If my friend Sumner could have known that I should have been asked to speak at his memorial service, he would not have died." And he resumed his seat. When, after the meeting, a friend spoke to him of the breathless silence which pervaded the audience, that they might catch every word, the poet quickly replied, "Do n't thee think they would have listened just as attentively if Balaam's animal had spoken?"

He was present at a lecture where the lecturer closed by repeating a passage from one of Mr. Whittier's poems. This was followed by an enthusiastic round of applause. Entirely unconscious that he had written it, he clapped vigorously with the others, and turning to a strange gentleman sitting by his side, inquired if he knew where the quotation came from. " Yes," said the gentleman ; " it is from one of Whittier's poems." — " Oh," he said, " the lecturer made it sound very well, did n't he ? "

One of the governors of Massachusetts said to Mr. Whittier, "I have taken my proclamation from King David and from you, Mr. Whittier." — "Well," responded the poet, " I do n't know that I have any objection ; but how about King David ? He might object to being in such company."

Some one asked his opinion of the Shakers. His reply was, "I do n't know anything about those dancing Dervishes. I do n't see any sense in such performances. I was always ashamed of King David for dancing before the Lord; and I never blamed his wife for being ashamed of him."

Mr. Whittier had keen pleasure in talking with his old neighbors, about the countryside, at the village store, or leaning against his own gate-posts. There was an old man whose original remarks greatly interested him; and he repeated to Mr. Emerson, one day, some of the quaint and wise sayings of his neighbor. Said Mr. Emerson: "That man ought to read Plato"; and he brought out a volume, and requested Mr. Whittier to hand it to him. This Mr. Whittier did on his return to Amesbury. His neighbor kept the volume for a while, and, on handing it back, said, "There are some good things in that book. I find this Mr. Plato has a good many of my idees."

There was an old man in his neighborhood, who had spent his life on a little farm with his wife, and his cow and his hens; at seventy years of age he and his wife converted the farm and the stock into money, and started to go round the world. He, with the coat he had worn for many years, unfaded only where the collar protected it from the sun and the storm; and the good wife with the same gown that had been made by the village dressmaker twenty years before, not in the least troubled that the sleeves were not in the latest fashion, and that the skirt did not dip in the back. They were gone a year. On their return, Mr. Whittier asked them about their journey. They had enjoyed it, they said; though the old man thought things were terribly out of repair over there in Europe, especially in Rome, and they did n't understand much about farming.

An old Quaker friend visited Mr. Whittier. He was a bachelor, and when the hour for retiring came, he was shown to his room. Soon after, he was heard calling from the top of the stairs in an excited tone, "I think thee has made a mistake, friend Whittier; I find *female* garments in my room."
At which friend Whittier replied, "Thee 'd better go to bed; the *female* garments won't hurt thee."

"In the days of witchcraft," he said, "I had an ancestor who helped to kill a witch. She and another woman got a lock of the witch's hair and put it in a hot oven and closed the oven door. Presently the most dreadful moans came from the oven, and repeated knocks and thumps against the door; but the good dames stoutly resisted the attacks with poker and tongs, keeping the oven tightly closed. Finally the sounds ceased, and in due time news came that the witch had died. This is the only connection I ever had with witches."

Mr. Whittier had some country neighbors who were Millerites. One, a woman, in explaining their belief, told her neighbor that the elect would be caught up on a cloud while the earth was purified by fire, then they would descend, and live on the earth, after it had been made fit for their habitation.

"Then," said the unbeliever, "thee will look down and see the fire consuming everything and everybody?"

"Yes."

"Well, for my part, I would rather be down here burning up than to sit up there on a damp cloud and see my neighbors burning."

A lady was one day bemoaning to Mr. Whittier her lack of means to live as she wished, and she closed by saying, "I fear I shall not have money enough left to bury me."

"My friend," quickly replied Mr. Whittier, "did thee ever know any one to stick by the way for lack of funds?"

Though his own dress was so plain he was very observant of the dress of others. He went one day to hear a woman read in public, and he said on his return, "———'s neck did n't look just right. Can't thee fix it up before she reads again? The lace appeared to fall down too much."

He was invited to a gathering of

literary people, and was asked by his hostess to take out to the dining-room a certain lady who was showily dressed. Her costume offended his sense of propriety, and he was very unhappy that he had to offer her his arm to go into the dining-room, where he dropped her as soon as possible, saying to his friend afterward, "I did n't care to take that woman on my arm; I think we must have cut a *pretty* figure, she with her fantastic gown, and I with my Quaker coat."

He told an amusing story of his mother who went by steamer with him to Portland.

"My mother," he said, "was not used to travelling by water, and she had a new Quaker bunnit made to go on her journey, and when we were well out to sea, she became very uncomfortable, and took off her new bunnit and placed it on a chair beside her. Her discomfort increased and she changed her position, forgetting where she had placed her new bunnit, and sat down on it; thee knows Quaker bunnits won't bear sitting on. This was too much for the good woman and she said, 'John, I want thee to take me right home.' — 'But,' said John, 'mother, we are way out to sea, I can't take thee home.' — 'Can't thee get the boat to turn round — I feel very sick, and my new bunnit will never do to wear to friend Smith's in Portland.' — 'No, mother, thee 'll have to make the best of it now.' — 'Oh, John, thee must never take me on the water again. I do'no as I shall live to get home.' "

He was often amused and sometimes annoyed by the foolish remarks made to him, and he said to me, " What does thee think women make such silly speeches to me for? It makes me feel like a fool. A woman said to me yesterday, 'Mr. Whittier, your smile is a benediction.' As I was walking across the floor at the Radical Club a woman stopped me in the middle of the parlor among all the folks, and said, 'I've long wished to see you, Mr. Whittier, to ask what you thought of the subjective and the objective.' Why, I thought the woman was crazy, and I said, 'I do n't know anything about either of 'em.'"

A young friend asked him one day if Mr. Fields's story were true about the woman who made her way to his library under pretence of conversing with him upon literary topics. "Mr. Fields said her conversation became very personal and tender, and you remarked, 'I do not understand thee, I do not understand thee; thee had better leave the room.' Was that really true, Mr. Whittier?" asked the young girl.

With a very funny twinkle in his eye, he replied, "Does thee think, Mary, I could treat a lady in so ungentlemanly a manner as that?"

That was the only response Mary could elicit.

He took great pleasure in talking with this young girl about the ways and doings of young people. He often said, "Come, sit thee down, and tell me about thy experiences since I last saw thee," to which Mary sometimes replied, "Mr. Whittier, you often ask me to tell you about my experiences, I think you ought to tell me some of yours."

"Well," said Mr. Whittier, "it is n't likely, Mary, that one has lived so long as I have in the world without having had some experiences, but it is n't worth while for an old man to talk much about them. Time was when I had my dreams and fancies — but those days have long since passed — do n't thee think I should have made a pretty good husband?"

"Yes," said Mary; "but I think if thee had wished to go to Amesbury on a certain train thee would have gone, wife or no wife."

At which reply he laughed a merry laugh, vigorously smote his knee, and said, "I guess thee is about right, Mary."

Shy as the poet was he was full of grace and delicate tact.

For a young girl, in whose love experiences he was much interested, he wrote the following little poem for her wedding day: —

EPITHALAMIUM.

We give to grace another home
The fairest of our flowers,

For love itself must yield to love
With stronger claim than ours.

Go, with our best hopes and our prayers,
A sweet and happy bride:
No path of life can lead astray
Where love alone is guide.

Go, rest thy heart upon a heart
And life with life ally:
That joy unshared is scarcely joy
Who better knows than I?

With thanks for all that thou hast been,
And trust for what shall be,
We fling our blessings, with our shoes,
For good luck after thee.

May health and plenty, love and friends,
With God's peace, make alway
For thee and thine the happiest home
By fair Sandusky's Bay!

On being asked for an autograph volume of his poems, for a fair which was being held for some charitable purpose, he wrote on the fly leaf —

> Not for the doubtful rhyme within
> Nor outside gold,
> Stranger or friend, I warn thee well,
> Should this be sold;
>
> But freely for the sake of such
> As homeless be,
> Give thrice its worth and it shall prove
> Cheap unto thee.
>
> Amesbury, 12th Mo., 1873.

In the winter of 1875, as some friends at whose house he had been a welcome and honored guest, were about sailing for Europe, he handed them an envelope saying, "I thought thee might like my autograph."

The contents were as follows: —

> "What shall I say, dear friends, to whom I owe
> The choicest blessings, dropping from the hands
> Of trustful love and friendship, as you go
> Forth on your journey to those elder lands,
> By saint and sage and bard and hero trod?

> Scarcely the simple farewell of the Friends
> Sufficeth : after you my full heart sends
> Such benediction as the pilgrim hears
> Where the Greek faith its golden dome uprears
> From Crimea's roses to Archangel snows
> The fittest prayer of parting : 'Go with God!'"

A friend of his youth, who had spent most of his life on the Illinois prairies, visited the poet, and together they recalled the scenes of their childhood, and briefly recounted the course of their after life. Whittier seemed much affected by the allusions of his friend to his prairie home, where a wife, children, and a grandchild, Constance, awaited his return; and on being asked for his autograph, replied, "Call on the way to the cars, and I will hand it to thee." The friend called and received the following :

> "The years that since we met have flown
> Leave, as they found me, still alone,
> Nor wife nor child nor grandchild dear
> Are mine, the heart of age to cheer.

More favored thou; with hair less gray
Than mine, can'st let thy fancy stray
To where thy little Constance sees
The prairie ripple in the breeze;
For one like her to lisp thy name
Is better than the voice of fame."

In an attempted visit to Hawthorne on one occasion, the scene which ensued must have been somewhat ludicrous. Mr. Whittier related it with great amusement. He said, "Thee knows I am not skilled in visits and small talk, but I wanted to make a friendly call on Hawthorne, and one morning — it chanced to be an ill-fated morning for this purpose — I sallied forth, and on reaching the house was ushered into a lugubrious-looking room where Hawthorne met me, evidently in a lugubrious state of mind.

"In rather a sepulchral tone of voice he bade me good-morning, and asked me to be seated opposite him, and we looked at each other and remarked upon the weather; then came an appalling silence and the cold chills crept down my back, and after a moment or two I got up and said, 'I think I will take a short walk.' I took my walk and returned to bid him good-morning, much to my relief, and I have no doubt to his."

In his last talk with Bishop Brooks, the two fell into a most cheerful conversation about the hopeful condition of the world. They were both full of hope and courage, and their hearty laughter rang through the house as they discussed the various questions that were in the air, and both agreed that they would like to live an hundred years to see the outcome of it all.

One day I invited some theological students from a school near by, wishing to give them the privilege of at least looking into the face of the poet beloved, but much doubting whether he would allow them to hear his voice. Fortunately the spirit stirred within him at sight of these embryo ministers who were soon to go out into the world to teach the people, and he opened his mouth and taught them such words of saintly wisdom as they had seldom heard. To this day they will bear testimony to the value of that golden hour, when, as from some old prophet, whose voice they had never heard, and would never hear again, they drank in the words that flowed from his lips when he taught them that life and love were so much more than any creeds of man's devising.

We thought it might be pleasant to him to meet his old anti-slavery associates, those with whom he labored in the early days of the Abolition warfare, and we invited all the "old war-horses" in the vicinity to meet him on a certain afternoon. The guests were all between seventy and ninety years of age and he said, "I guess thee never saw such a lot of old cronies together before. There is B——, thee must n't forget him, and there is ——, he was a great fighter, he must be asked. There 's so and so, he is a good deal of a crank, but he must n't be left out." It was delightful to see him with his old friends, with whom he stood shoulder to shoulder in the great struggle, and hear them recount the stirring events of the times that tried men's souls. He said, "Do n't thee think we are pretty cheerful martyrs?"

When the excitement of the hour was at its height all tongues were silenced by the voice of a woman singing "John Brown's body," all eyes were turned toward the piano where the singer was seated playing her own accompaniment. She was one of the "unfortunate race," and as her thrilling tones, tremulous with emotion, floated through the rooms, every voice caught up the song, — those who had a voice to sing, and those who sang with their souls, swelled the grand chorus, and at the conclusion there was not a dry eye in the room.

"Who is that woman with the wonderful voice?" asked one of the guests.

"She was a *slave*" — was the reply.

Mr. Whittier listened with bowed head, his eyes suffused with tears, and his flushed cheeks showing the deepest emotion.

During the afternoon, in the midst of the festivities, for it was really quite a festive company, notwithstanding some of the guests were fourscore and ten, an old man covered with the dust of travel, and bowed with the weight of years, walked into their midst and said, "I am a stranger; I have heard since I arrived in this city that John G. Whittier was in this house; I have travelled two hundred and fifty miles, all the way from York State, to see him."

The old man was courteously received, and was asked to take a seat. Mr. Whittier was pointed out to him, and he sought a position where he could keep his eye on the object of his search every moment. Towards the close of the afternoon, as he arose to take his departure, having scarcely spoken from the time he entered the room, he said, "I have journeyed a long distance to see John G. Whittier. I have seen him and I have seen much more than I expected.

I should be happy and ready to go home if I could have his autograph."

Mr. Whittier ran upstairs like an antelope, excited by the companionship of his old friends, wrote his name and brought it to the old man, who took it and scanning it with wondering eyes, turned to the hostess as if the favor were too great for him, and said, "Do you *really* think he wrote that?" Upon being assured the poet really wrote it he departed on his homeward way entirely satisfied.

Mrs. Child was one of the guests. After the company had left, Mr. Whittier said, "Liddy had something new on her bunnit. She has worn that bunnit for ten years, but she had some new fixin' on it to-day. What does thee think it was? What does thee think she carries in that bag she always keeps so close to her? I have never seen her without it by her side, hugging it as if it contained some precious treasure."

He often remarked that Mrs. Child was ostracized in the early days on account of her anti-slavery principles. "No woman in this country," said he, "has sacrificed so much for principle as Mrs. Child. She gave promise in early life of great literary ability, but when she espoused the cause of the Abolitionists she found no market for her books and essays, and her praises were suddenly silenced."

Mrs. Child retired early from the world, and she was as shy and retiring as Mr. Whittier. It was hard to induce her to leave the privacy of her own home. She was invited one day to the house where Mr. Whittier was being entertained, with the promise that no one else should be present, if she would come and spend the day with her old friend; but meeting a mutual friend of theirs, one who had labored and fought with them both through all the years of the anti-slavery struggle, their hostess ventured to ask him to join the company. Before the day came, the friend, unfortunately, met Mrs. Child, and expressed regret that he should not be able to meet her on the following day, as he greatly desired to do. Mrs. Child immediately wrote a characteristic note saying, "The cat is out of the bag. When Quakers and Methodists put their heads together to deceive the very elect — I do n't know what the world is coming to. Are there any more cats in that bag?"

Mr. Whittier's letters were not literary productions, looking to his biographer; but, though often containing brief allusions to State or national affairs, they were commonly personal messages, instinct with the feeling of the moment, describing his own condition of health, and expressing interest in, or affection for, the one to whom he wrote. This native shyness and modesty led him to speak always with gratitude, and often with surprise, of the attentions that were showered upon him.

His letters were only second in interest to his visits; they breathed the same spirit of modest reserve and affectionate interest that were prominent in his conversation. He wrote : —

"I will tell thee now what I could not say to thee at thy house, that I enjoyed every moment of my long visit. Of the special kindness with which I was received into thy household circle, I can only say that I wish that I deserved it."

"And now Emerson has passed on! How the great and good are leaving us. There is nothing now for us but to love God, and good men, and one another more."

In reply to an invitation to visit Oak Bluff, at a time when General Grant was to be there, he says, "What with the camp meetings and General Grant, I really do n't dare to undertake it. I do n't want to see camp meetings, and I do n't want to run after General Grant. There will be a grand row on the Island, and a Quaker would be miserably out of place."

"I was in Boston last week, and stopped at the Marlboro, but I am afraid my pleasant sojourn in Mt. Vernon Street has made me a little fastidious as to my lodgings. I passed by thy house as Ossian passed by the walls of Balclutha, and found them desolate. It would have been so pleasant, just to step in and sit by thy cheerful hearth."

Speaking of a politician of whom he did not approve: "I should n't wonder if he were willing to sell out. He had not much character to lose, and what little he had was hardly worth the trouble of keeping."

"I am made happy by thy note, inviting me to thy pleasant home, for it assures me that I am not an unwelcome guest; and yet I sometimes wonder at the kindness which throws open such homes to me. I do n't think I deserve it, but I am very glad and thankful nevertheless."

"They do n't break roads in Danvers. It is a marvellously white world that I

look out upon. The sunsets are superb, and the moonlight photographs of trees on the lawn are very beautiful. Nothing can be finer than the level sun at setting streaming through the western pines, and the violet-tinted hills on the horizon, in contrast with the golden sky above, and the white snow below them. But, after all, I think Boston, with such a southern exposure and cheerful outlook as thee have in Mt. Vernon Street, is more satisfactory in winter. So I hope to look in upon thee soon."

"October, 1880. — Was there ever such an October? Such color, such late bloom (or blaze) of flowers, such a heavenly atmosphere!"

"Take sin out of this world, and it would be good enough for me."

"I have heard my friend may go to Washington, and I should go for it but for one thing, — thee would shut thy pleasant home in Mt. Vernon Street, — what then should I do?"

"I suppose Butler is destined to be thy colleague; and if he wants to carry his point with thee, he will take thee on thy weak side of Methodism, as he did in the case of the young Christian soldier of the Custom House."

"As, with the years, the circle of my limitations narrows about me, I am obliged to give up a great many things; but my love and regard for my friends is none the less strong, that I cannot see them as frequently as I could wish."

"I never saw the orchard so beautiful as now; and my heart is full of thankfulness that I am spared to enjoy the wonderful beauty."

To some friends who were travelling abroad he wrote: —

"AMESBURY, 6th Mo., 7, 1875. — I wish I could have been with thee in Florence, and I should have been glad to have been with Governor Claflin when he visited Kossuth.

"Thee must now, I think, be in England amidst its historic towers and its eye-satisfying greenness. Thee will see Wordsworth's lakes and mountains, and thee will go to Scotland, and walk the paths worn by the feet of Burns and Scott, and thee will have a good time of it, and all thy friends will be glad for thy sake. I am going to send thee the likeness of an old Quaker friend of thine; it is all I have to send. Thy assured friend, J. G. W."

"JUNE. — Summer is here at last, and our bleak and hard New England lovely with the sober, persistent beauty which becomes her. I am glad the dreadful east winds are getting their icy wings melted, as I have suffered greatly from them."

"Amesbury, 7th Mo., 1881. — Miss Freeman's speech was eloquent and wise — the best thing in the Institute. Perhaps even Francis Parkman might think she could be safely trusted to vote."

After writing a pleasant letter, full of sweet expressions of friendship, he says, "I look back with pleasure to my somewhat protracted visit — a pleasure not unmingled with a feeling of regret that it is passed — a memory and not an anticipation. I miss the kind faces at thy breakfast table, and I saw by the newspaper that I was visiting 'The Old Elms,' and from my heart I wished the paper told the truth. The papers have made me ubiquitous this summer. I have been at two or three places at the same time."

"OAK KNOLL, 10th Mo., 15, 1880. — Dear friend: — All's well! We can see light now and are out of the Maine woods. I must reach out and shake hands with thee over the victories of Ohio and Indiana. They are so decisive that they have settled the presidential question, and I am very thankful. Of course, I take it for granted the Republicans will not relax their efforts; New York and New Jersey must be had, and I think we can have them by hard work.

"How comfortable it is to have Blank out of our way and bottled up in the Democracy."

"I have seen a portrait of Mohini, the young Brahmin. He has a beautiful face. It seems like a spirit's. I hear he told some of his agnostic hearers that they could have no guide and master better than Jesus Christ, and some of them, I hear, have bought a Bible."

One has said — I would rather give a man or a woman on the verge of a great moral lapse a marked copy of Whittier, than any other book in our language. Apropos of this, not long since a delicate, high-strung girl in college, overwrought with the strain of examinations and the difficulties of her new life, went to the president, and said, "It is of no use, I cannot go on, my life is a failure; I must leave college and go home."

The tactful president replied, "Go to the library and take Whittier's poems, sit down by your window and read 'The Grave by the Lake,' then come and I will talk with you."

The young girl came back in an hour with a changed countenance. She said, "I will overcome the obstacles, I will go on with my college course. I believe, after reading Whittier, that life is worth the effort."

In one of our prisons there was a woman who seemed utterly callous to every good influence. It seemed as if the very spirits of the evil world had taken possession of her, and those about her had apparently no influence over her. One day, after a paroxysm of temper, when she was more like a wild animal than a human being, the superintendent handed her a volume of Whittier's poems, and asked her to sit quietly down and read "The Eternal Goodness." Returning, after a half hour, the superintendent found the poor, half-crazed creature still reading, her wild eyes softened with tears, and she said in subdued tones, "That is beautiful reading, but is it true what it says? Does God love *me?*" Often afterward she was found poring over the book, and her improvement dated from that hour.

> "Still Thy love, O Christ arisen,
> Yearns to reach these souls in prison!
> Through all depths of sin and loss
> Drops the plummet of Thy cross!
> Never yet abyss was found
> Deeper than that cross could sound!"

An eminent author once said, "I would crawl on my hands and knees till I sank, if I could write a book that the plain people would read and love." This Whittier has done.

If the worth of a life may be estimated by the number of hearts comforted, the number of lives uplifted and inspired, Mr. Whittier's measure will exceed that of most men of this or any other century. "He has given us the poetry of human brotherhood and human purity. He has given us a Christ-like example. He has sung to us of faith in God and immortality."

The beautiful life finished its earthly course on a perfect summer's morning, and he entered the life for which he longed. His last words were characteristic. He was breathing out his life; his eyes were closed, and his friends stood around the bed about which had clustered so much loving interest, waiting and watching for the last look, or the last word, when he opened those eyes which had often seemed to look into the mysteries of eternity, and said with labored breath: "My — love — to — the — world."

This was the last message from the great heart that had served the world so faithfully, and to whom, if love is the chief charm of heaven, the circumstance of death will make little difference.

No church was large enough to contain the friends who came together on the day of his burial. They gathered in his own garden under the trees he loved; and through the quivering leaves the sunshine glimmered, and the soft breeze sighed, as they paid their last tribute of respect and affection to him who lay, almost buried in flowers, while the waiting thousands passed the bier to look upon his transfigured face.

"And so the shadows fall apart,
And so the west winds play,
And all the windows of my heart I open to the
    day."

Amidst silence broken only by sobs, a dear Quaker friend, whose serene and spiritual appearance was in accord with the solemn scene, arose, and in a calm, sweet voice repeated one of his last songs : —

"No gate of pearl, no branch of palm I merit,
Nor street of shining gold —

* * * * *

Some humble door among thy many mansions,
　Some sheltering shade where sin and striving cease,
And flows forever through heaven's green expansions
　The river of thy peace.
There, from the music round about me stealing,
　I fain would learn the new and holy song,
And find at last, beneath thy trees of healing,
　The life for which I long."

www.ingramcontent.com/pod-product-compliance
Lightning Source LLC
Chambersburg PA
CBHW031120160426
43192CB00008B/1055